WRITERS' WORKSHOP SERIES

GU01007410

How to teach fiction writing at key stage 3

NEIL MACRAE

David Fulton Publishers
London

David Fulton Publishers Ltd
The Chiswick Centre, 414 Chiswick High Road, London W4 5TF

www.fultonpublishers.co.uk

First published in Great Britain by David Fulton Publishers 2002

British Library Cataloguing in Publication Data
A catalogue record for this book is available from the British Library.

ISBN 1-85346-858-4

Also available in the **Writers' Workshop Series:**

Acknowledgements:

The publishers would like to thank the following copyright holders for permission to include their material:

United Media Inc., for *Peanuts* cartoon strip. Reproduced by permission. © United Media, 1969.

Oxford University Press, for 'Gran's Last Journey', from *Short!* by Kevin Crossley-Holland. Reproduced by permission.

Portobello Pictures Ltd, for the still from *Danny, The Champion of the World.*

Topham Picturepoint, for fashion photos (p. 58) and abandoned farm (p. 61).

Every effort has been made to contact copyright holders. We apologise for any inadvertent omissions, and invite copyright holders to contact us with any information which should be included in future editions of this book.

Illustrations © Sarah Wimperis 2002, Graham-Cameron Illustration
Page design by Ken Vail Graphic Design
Cover photographs by John Redman
Typeset by FiSH Books, London
Printed in Great Britain by Bell and Bain Ltd, Glasgow

Contents

Introduction

This book is for *all* those at work in the classroom who talk about, read and write stories. The book assumes that both teachers and pupils will be actively engaged in the process of story writing – finding ways to make the story-writing experience come alive through working together.

Much of the text of the book is addressed to those who will be writing the stories. Most of the time this will be pupils in the classroom – but not always! There are some notes for teachers too and these focus on how the work can be best managed. Much of this work will be differentiated by outcome but, where there are opportunities for different approaches to the activities, these will be indicated.

How to use this book – for teachers

Whilst the book is based on the good practice that is found in the *Key Stage 3 Framework for the Teaching of English* (2000), it can be used flexibly to develop different aspects of narrative writing. The reader will not find key objectives attached to each workshop, but the language of the *Framework* will often be referred to and can be clearly seen in the text. The book is also linked with requirements of the new *National Curriculum for English* (1999) and the demands of the Key Stage 3 SATs.

How to Teach Fiction Writing at Key Stage 3 could be used as the basis for a series of schemes of work across the key stage. The progressive development of a range of skills is matched to the demands of the *Framework* and teachers may find that they could present the workshops as part of their schemes of work in Years 7 to 9.

The book is based on the key premise that linking the imagination to the development of skills must go hand in hand in order to create good writing. The book is presented as a practical manual to help teachers in the classroom. It recognises that the National Literacy Strategy focus on effective modelling and scaffolding strategies can support the secure development of young writers. The teaching structure described in the *Key Stage 3 Framework for the Teaching of English* provides a clear focus for how this can be followed in the classroom. An outline of the structure is shown below. Teachers should:

- Establish clear aims.
- Provide examples for pupils.
- Explore the features of the text.
- Define the conventions.
- Demonstrate how the text is written.
- Compose some text together.
- Scaffold the first attempts.
- Allow pupils to write independently.
- Draw out key learning.

It is worth adding three further points to this list.

First, this is *not* a lesson structure. It would be difficult (and possibly undesirable) to try and achieve all these objectives in the course of one lesson – however long! Things need to happen between the elements of this process. Pupils need to talk about what they are doing, and reflect on what they have understood and written. Talking about the writing produced is highlighted at every stage in each of the six chapters of *How to Teach Fiction Writing at Key Stage 3*.

Second, it is important that the finished narratives have an audience that is more than just the classroom teacher or the story writer. Publishing and displaying, sending to newspapers, reading aloud to a new audience, and developing into other formats are all possibilities.

Third, *How to Teach Fiction Writing at Key Stage 3* recognises the demands and limitations of work in the classroom. Novelists and screenwriters spend months and years on their stories – but in the classroom we simply don't have that kind of time. So there is an unashamed focus in this book on the short story in all its different forms. This is intended to be both pragmatic and stimulating.

For teachers and pupils, there is rarely enough time in the classroom to support the writing of long stories. Nonetheless, many pupils like to do this, and teachers should provide encouragement, support and guidance for developing authors.

As a pupil, the requirement to create a long story can often be very demanding. In this book there is a clear premise – great stories can be short! The narrative ideas that form the basis of many stories (in print and on screen) are often very simple: it is the complexity chosen by the writer that characterises the story and defines its qualities.

How the book is organised

The book is divided into six 'chapters', each containing linked narrative writing activities that focus on:

- genre conventions
- the craft of the writer
- some specific year-related needs derived from the *Framework*
- a step by step approach that uses the convention of word-, sentence- and text-level thinking
- some examples of writing from well-known writers
- visual links to the related narrative forms and conventions, e.g. films, advertising and television.

Each series of activities build up to a more substantial narrative writing task. Teachers could use these tasks as key assessed pieces. It is intended that the chapters form self-contained units of writing across the three years of the key stage. The needs of both the most and the least able are addressed in each of the chapters.

Telling stories

Telling stories – or making narratives – is a basic instinct for all of us. We tell stories all the time to make patterns in our lives that usually aren't really there. Our lives make more sense to us when we can create order.

Tell the truth about this one: how often have you added just that little bit more to your telling of something true that happened to you to make it more interesting, more believable – or even more unbelievable?

Of course you have.

We all do this. Take it too far and it can get you into serious trouble – or help start a career as a storyteller...We must use this skill wisely. This book is about how to develop the skills that make stories work.

How to use the Activities

The aim of this book is simple and straightforward – it will help you to become a better, more confident fiction writer. You will probably have spent time focusing on improving your writing skills at Key Stage 2. *How to Teach Fiction Writing at Key Stage 3* takes these skills forward in your work in the secondary school. The book is divided into six chapters, each one covering a new aspect of writing fiction. Each chapter builds on the last one, so it is useful to go through the chapters in the right order.

Where stories come from

The book assumes that fiction stories – or narratives – can be developed from all sorts of starting points. Here are just a few of the many sources that can be used. Some of them are used in this book.

> overheard conversations, incidents in school, radio news items, short stories and novels we read, things that happen to us, poems we read, funny stories in newspapers, family stories about ourselves and others, urban legends, mini-sagas, television advertisements, jokes we are told, magazine articles, films we see...

All media forms provide us with sources that we can raid to create our new stories. Writers know that ideas have to come from somewhere and that the key is to tap into as many sources of ideas as possible. This book encourages that process.

Telling stories

Telling stories – or making narratives – is a basic instinct for all of us. We tell stories all the time to make patterns in our lives that usually aren't really there. Our lives make more sense to us when we can create order.

Tell the truth about this one: how often have you added just that little bit more to your telling of something true that happened to you to make it more interesting, more believable – or even more unbelievable?

Of course you have.

We all do this. Take it too far and it can get you into serious trouble – or help start a career as a storyteller... We must use this skill wisely. This book is about how to develop the skills that make stories work.

Before you begin – making narratives

Telling stories – or making narratives – is a basic instinct for all of us.

I use these two words – story and narrative – to mean the same thing. Do these words have the same meaning or is there a difference between them?

In some dictionaries they may be presented as synonyms (words that mean the same), but the French writer Gérard Genette gave them two clear and different meanings. These are helpful when we are writing, so here I use Genette's definitions.

We often think of a story as a tale with the events told in the order in which they happened – in chronological order. In a traditional fairy tale this might typically be shown by:

> 'Once upon a time . . .' at the start of the tale, through to 'and they all lived happily ever after' at the end.

Genette called this linear narrative *histoire*, or story. But, of course, the sequence of events that make up this story could be rearranged in many different ways – a different sequence, told by a different character and so on. Genette says that this needs a different term – he calls this *récit*, or narrative.

So, the raw material of a story (histoire) will come to us in one particular version – a narrative (récit). This is an important idea: the same basic story can have all sorts of narrative forms and so the possibilities are endless. This also reminds us that we can re-order the events in a story to suit our purposes. It is exciting when, as writers, we first try the techniques of flashback and anticipation. Both of these approaches are covered in the Activities you will be working on.

Throughout, I will use the word *story* to describe the raw material that a wide range of *narratives* can be made into.

© Neil MacRae ISBN 1-85346-858-4

1 'One dark and stormy night...'

National Curriculum Framework links

Y7 – Writing

- *plan, draft, edit, revise, proofread and present a text with readers and purpose in mind*
- *collect, select and assemble ideas in a suitable planning format, e.g. flow chart, list, star chart*
- *use writing to explore and develop ideas, e.g. journals, brainstorm techniques and mental mapping activities*
- *structure a story with an arresting opening, a developing plot, a complication, a crisis and satisfying resolution.*

Y8 – Study of literary texts

- *recognise the conventions of some common literary form, e.g. sonnet, and genres, e.g. Gothic horror, and explore how a particular text adheres to or deviates from established conventions.*

Pupil support

This unit focuses on plot. It's what pupils want to get right and what is often most difficult. Pupils may use plots derived from a number of sources and sometimes these are inappropriate for the very short story. The reasons why this happens are discussed in the pupil notes for Chapter 6, where plot is explored again in more detail.

Some pupils will have explored aspects of genre conventions at KS2. They can be reminded of this knowledge before beginning Activity 2. Ensure that this knowledge is shared with the whole group. Don't let pupils get bogged down in plot details – focus the brainstorming on individual words and phrases. Assist with extracts from typical mystery stories if appropriate. These A4 brainstorms could be enlarged to A3 and displayed in the classroom.

For Activity 4, the whole cartoon strip has been provided as an A4 page so that the text can be presented as an OHT.

When working on Activity 7, teachers should beware of the tyranny of the continuous prose draft. To have text 'set in stone' in this way can make it difficult to see where modification can be made. Teachers marking such material may not be able to offer much guidance beyond the technical because it is difficult to make structural changes in an already set format.

Teachers can help pupils get the note-taking structure right before making any notes on the narrative. Providing some kind of visual or diagrammatic structure to support the completion of the narrative will be useful here.

A writing frame can be presented as a series of boxes in an A4 user-friendly landscape format, showing the components of the narrative – the genre that has been chosen, the opening sentence(s), the ending of the narrative and three paragraph boxes. This will be particularly useful for less able pupils.

Activity 1

Introducing genre

Have a look at the first frame from this *Peanuts* cartoon.

Snoopy has obviously got to take his narrative from there so where do you think it is going? What would your next few lines be as a writer?

Write down some thoughts individually and then share and compare with a partner. Note these in the box below or in your workbook.

Can you begin to describe the *type* of story you have started? Does it fit into any particular kind of story that you know? If it does, we can probably tell the type or *genre* of the story already – horror, science fiction, western, romance and so on. The opening 'It was a dark and stormy night' suggests a horror or mystery story – is this what you have written?

Talk to your partner about the story you have started. Put any comments about the *type* of story in the box below or in your workbook.

Activity 2

'I wonder what could be in that cave?' said Alex

With your partner, identify some typical features of a mystery story. Where might it be set? What kinds of characters would you expect to meet? What sorts of events are likely to take place? What are the likely names for people and places in your narrative?

Brainstorm some ideas about each of these aspects. Choose a genre (from Chapter 1, Activity 1) and put it into the circle. Note down your ideas under the headings in the boxes.

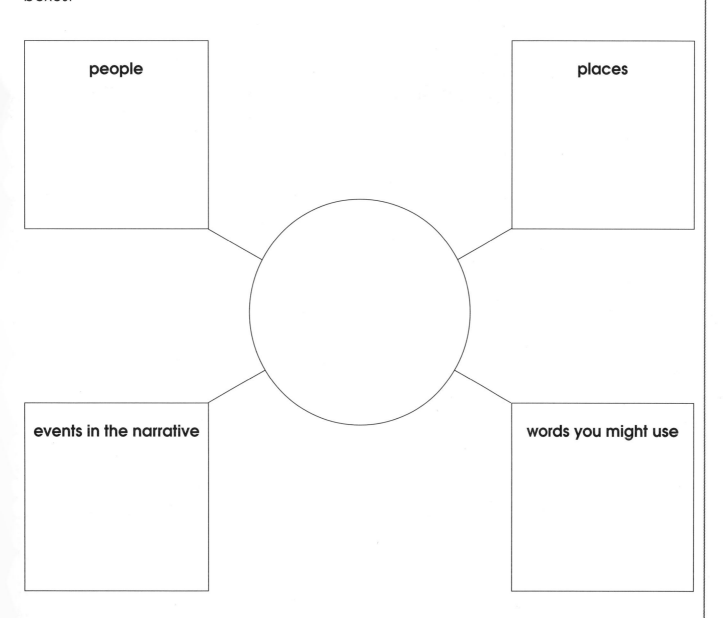

people

places

events in the narrative

words you might use

Keep the ideas you develop – they will be useful later on! Put this information in your workbook or display the brainstormed ideas in your classroom.

Activity 3

'Suddenly a shot rang out.'

Here's what Snoopy produced to follow that first sentence:

It's easy to see what has gone wrong here. Can you describe the kind of stories that each of the sentences suggests?

'The maid screamed' and 'Suddenly a pirate ship appeared on the horizon' belong to very different kinds of story. In what kinds of story and where in the story would these two sentences appear?

Discuss this with your partner.

© Neil MacRae ISBN 1-85346-858-4

Activity 4

'I may have written myself into a corner.'

Unfortunately, Snoopy continued to create problems for himself by writing more sentences that come from different genres. If you haven't read narratives that would contain these kinds of sentences, can you imagine them as part of what might happen in a film or television programme?

Look closely at the frames of the complete cartoon. Working with a partner, outline the kinds of narrative that might come from each of these sentences. Use the diagram from Activity 2 to help you. Share your thinking with other pairs.

Snoopy had no idea of where his narrative was going. Without some ideas about what genre of story he wanted to write, or how it might develop, he was bound to write himself into that corner.

Activity 5

Genre survey

Surveys among young writers show that some genres are more popular than others. When Elaine Millard did some research with 80 young writers (40 boys and 40 girls) she discovered that horror stories were the most popular. Here are the different genres that she came across in her research:

horror   adventure   teen   children's   war

science fiction   detective   school   sport

folk   ghost   western   parody

Which genres are most popular with your friends? Discuss the kinds of genres you tend to write in. Are there others you would add to this list? Is there any debate about some kinds of stories? Is a hospital setting a new kind of genre or is it little different from other stories set in a particular place – a prison or a school? Do we tend to find the same kinds of plots and characters in these settings? Discuss what would be the typical features of this genre. Think about television programmes and films too.

Share your ideas with a larger group and discuss the conclusions you come to. Remember that there are no right answers here: genres change and develop over time.

© Neil MacRae ISBN 1-85346-858-4

Activity 6

It starts like this ...

In the previous five Activities of Chapter 1, you have been developing your understanding about a range of different fiction. In each genre we might have the same sort of story structure.

The most basic form of narrative will look like this:

Orientation	The writer sets the scene: we meet a main character; we find out when and where the narrative is set; some details of the setting may give us clues about what will happen next. We find out what kind of story is being told from clues the writer gives to us.
Complication	Something happens involving the main character. This might stop them doing what they want to do but they find a way around the problem. If they are good, then they will overcome the problem because of their qualities; if they are bad, then they may cheat or do something wrong.
Resolution	The complication is resolved – either happily or unhappily. Sometimes the ending is not clear but we can guess what might happen from clues that we have been given in the narrative. If there is a 'twist' at the end, there will usually be clues too.

Does this read like some stories you know? Test out the pattern on some story ideas you know. Think about both the way the plot of the story is organised and the ways in which the characters are used.

Note down some of the ideas in the box below or in your workbook.

Activity 7

Getting going on a narrative

Your work so far still doesn't give you much to write about. To make sure that this first narrative is successful, you will need some ideas to get you started. Remember that writers are good at stealing ideas – so steal one of the ideas below!

Working on your own, select just **one** of these story ideas:

> Two characters have always disliked each other. An incident in which they are competing unexpectedly brings them together. They realise that their dislike of each other was based on a misunderstanding.

> The main character has to look after something very valuable. Something happens to the object, but a replacement is finally found. The owner of the object finds out. What is their reaction?

> The opposite of the previous outline: the main character finds an object. It isn't quite what it appears to be and the object must (reluctantly) be given up. How does the main character feel about this – are they relieved or not?

> Finally, something more specific. A boy or girl has always wished to own a pet. An opportunity to have an unusual pet comes up but there's a twist... Does the story end happily or unhappily? If the child in your narrative has made no mistakes, it would normally end happily – but...

© Neil MacRae ISBN 1-85346-858-4

Activity 7 (continued)

To help you focus on how your narrative is going to develop, follow these basic rules:

- Think about the genre you have chosen for your narrative.

- Plan the ending of your narrative now!

- Have an opening that will make the reader want to read on.

- Limit yourself to just two different locations.

- Write three paragraphs – one for each of section of the narrative.

- Add more paragraphs *only* if you really need them (you might include some key conversation, for example).

- Don't worry about developing characters very much.

- Keep your narrative to no more than 250 words!

Think about using some of the ideas you have generated in the previous Activities. Don't expect that your narrative will be perfect when you have completed the 250 words. This doesn't matter!

Activity 8

Reshaping and refining

When you have written your 250-word narrative, show the text to a partner and use the key questions below to help you discuss any improvements that might be made.

- Was the ending planned? Does it relate well to the opening of the story?

- Do we get an idea of what your character(s) is like from what they do?

- Is the location or setting of the story used usefully? Does it influence what happens?

- Does the story have some suspense?

- Does the reader want to find out about what happened?

Now, revise the elements of your narratives and compare with others. What have you learned from this process?

Note down up to *five* things that will help you write a better narrative next time. Write down this information in the box below or in your workbook.

© Neil MacRae ISBN 1-85346-858-4

2 A story in 50 words? Impossible...

National Curriculum Framework links

Y7 – Understanding the author's craft

- *comment, using appropriate terminology, on how writers convey setting, character and mood through word choice and sentence structure*
- *trace the ways in which a writer structures a text to prepare a reader for the ending, and comment on the effectiveness of the ending.*

Y8 – Writing

- *experiment with different approaches to planning, drafting, proofreading and presenting writing, taking account of the time available*
- *re-read work to anticipate the effect on the reader and revise style and structure, as well as accuracy, with this in mind.*

Pupil support

Activity 1 illustrates how the use of individual words can modify and change emphasis. It will be important to ensure that pupils know why 'the' is more powerful than 'a' in this context.

Discuss, exchange and display the responses to *The door slammed!* The aim here is to develop further the culture of collaborative writing – writing in the classroom is not necessarily a solitary activity. Teacher modelling of a good follow-on from this dramatic opening sentence would be very effective at this point – and encouragement for pupil modelling (through use of an OHT or mini-whiteboards) would extend the role of collaboration.

To support Activity 2, teachers could collect opening sentences from texts at home, in the school library, etc. These can then be discussed/analysed and annotated to show the effects that contribute to the arresting quality of the opening. The best of these can be presented as enlarged annotated examples around the classroom, illustrating arresting starting points.

Additionally, teachers can challenge pupils to make up their own effective opening sentences and encourage responses from other pupils. The aim is to see and understand the techniques and ways in which writers achieve their effects and to ensure that all pupils can participate in discussion about these techniques.

Guy Carter's prizewinning mini-saga in Activity 4 makes us think. The writer is giving us a message. Right from the opening word *Friendless*, the writer is sending a clear message about how life has changed over the centuries and what it will become in the future. Explore with pupils how this mini-saga achieves its complex effects.

Mini-sagas require precision editing. Because of this they are perfect for completion on a word processor. Two key points for teachers to remember when supporting work on Activity 5 are:

- Using the word-count facility saves laborious counting by hand. The opportunity to move text around, cut and paste and use the thesaurus facility all enhance the creative experience.
- Revising the text with a partner is most productive using a shared computer screen.

Activity 1

Make every word count

The narrative that you've written (and revised) in Chapter 1, Activities 7 and 8, is a *very* short story. It may be the first time that you have tried to write to such a tight structure. It might have felt awkward or difficult to do. Some writers have become real experts in writing the very short story and in this chapter you will learn about how they make their narratives work.

Remember Snoopy's opening sentences? Some worked and some didn't. One that did was 'A door slammed.' It might have been even better as 'The door slammed!'

Look closely at the two sentences:

> A door slammed.
>
> The door slammed.

Which one works best? Can you work out why?

Write down some thoughts in the box below or in your workbook.

Compare your views with those of others. Any conclusions?

 © Neil MacRae ISBN 1-85346-858-4

Activity 1 (continued)

Now try the best of the two sentences as an opening sentence for a narrative. Develop your opening in three *different* ways by writing a short paragraph for each narrative idea. You might try three different genres and see what happens. Look back at the list in Activity 5 if you need to. Use the starter sheet provided to start you off.

Compare some of the ideas you have developed. How did the opening sentence help you? Look at the paragraphs others have written. What makes them work?

> The door slammed! Kathy whirled round but she could see nothing. She tried the brass door handle but the door was now firmly locked. Outside, the rain pattered against the tiny window. Kathy sank slowly to the floor, her head in her hands.

The door slammed!

The door slammed!

The door slammed!

Activity 2

It all began when...

Look at these three opening sentences and discuss what makes them work:

> John looked at his watch: he would be twelve years old in exactly twelve hours time.

> 'I wonder where that gerbil has got to?' said Jackie's mother.

> At first glance, the little bungalow seemed ordinary enough.

Now look at these comments about the three sentences:

Opening 1

Starting with a *pattern* can be intriguing – the reader wants to see how the pattern will be used later on in the story.

Opening 2

A *question* is always a good start because we know that in some way the question will be answered if we read on.

Opening 3

Using a word that *signals* what is happening – here it is the 'magic' word '*seemed*' – can tell us so much about the kind of narrative we have just started. What does 'seemed' mean here? What is the writer telling us?

© Neil MacRae ISBN 1-85346-858-4

Activity 3

In the beginning was...

Some writers have created opening sentences that are as famous now as when they were first written:

> 'There's no such thing as the perfect murder,' Tom said to Reeves.
>
> Patricia Highsmith, *Ripley's Game*

> It was a bright cold day in April, and the clocks were striking thirteen.
>
> George Orwell, *1984*

> Last night I dreamt I went to Manderley again.
>
> Daphne du Maurier, *Rebecca*

Now look at some more opening sentences from stories for young people:

> It seemed to Catherine that from the moment they set out on their journey she knew it was going to be a very special one.
>
> Berlie Doherty, *Children of Winter*

> Johnny never knew for certain why he started seeing the dead.
>
> Terry Pratchett, *Johnny and the Dead*

> There is no lake at Camp Green Lake.
>
> Louis Sacher, *Holes*

How do these six opening sentences work? Talk with your partner about what you think of when you read them. Have you come across any other good ones that you can remember? You're not going to develop this story idea any further, but the discussion might have given you some ideas that you want to think about for later. Jot them down now in the box below or in your workbook.

Activity 4

Mini-sagas 1 Fifty golden words

The mini-saga is a recent invention. It was started by the *Daily Telegraph* newspaper and followed up by the BBC, who broadcast the results on the radio.

The name is really a joke. Originally, sagas were long stories of dramatic events over many generations, told by Norse and Icelandic peoples. They were probably started to provide entertainment around the fire during the long winter nights in those countries. Today we gather round the television and watch soap operas which tell long stories of dramatic events over many generations...

A mini-saga must be exactly fifty words long and it must be a real story. The title is very important so the rule is that any title can be up to fifteen words long.

The limitation of fifty words means that the mini-saga writer needs to think very imaginatively about just what words are really necessary to tell the story.

Read these mini-sagas on the next page, written by young people, and work out how they create their effects.

The final example, 'The Postcard', is an adult mini-saga – a winner of the *Daily Telegraph* mini-saga competition. What do you think made it stand out and eventually win from over 48,000 entries?

The Death Touch!

When a daughter went away to college, she reluctantly left her plants and her goldfish in her mother's care. Once, the daughter telephoned and her mother confessed that the plants and the goldfish had died. There was a prolonged silence. Finally, in a small voice, the daughter asked, 'How's Dad?'

Dawn Hunt

Silence in Court

The jury watches as the frightened girl slowly walks up to the witness stand. She is only eleven years old, and doesn't like what she sees. As the questions are asked, she tries to answer, but tears stream down her face. It's not easy being witness to a murder.

Debby Dell

Who Dares Wins

He was scared. It was his first drop. The transport shuddered violently on its journey through the night. They were over the dropping-zone. Soon it would be knives into unsuspecting bodies. Killing silently. 'Ready?' said the Sergeant. 'Go.' He said a prayer and jumped into the streets of Troy.

N M Cooper

Friend

Tumbling and rolling beneath the warm Pacific, my friend and I plunge past the beautiful coral, our fins skimming the sand. My stomach turns as I hear my friend scream in panic. I look around to see him caught in a tuna net. And they say that dolphins can't cry . . .

Claire Clark

The Postcard

Friendless, he despatched a letter to the twelfth century. Illuminated scrolls arrived by return post. Jottings to Tutankahmen secured hieroglyphics on papyrus; Hannibal sent a campaign report. But when he addressed the future, hoping for cassettes crammed with wonders, a postcard drifted back with scorched edges. It glowed all night.

Guy Carter

Talk to a partner about why/how these mini-sagas work. Each example creates their effects in different ways – can you see what these are? Discuss with a partner and note down your comments.

Activity 5

Mini-sagas 2 From 18 to 24 carat

Now for a challenge.

The mini-saga below is still in its first draft form. The writer has concentrated on getting his fifty words – but are they the *best* fifty words he could use? What advice would you give this young writer on how to improve his writing? Think of some ideas yourself and then share them with a partner.

The Train Crash

I was travelling on a train to Glasgow to see my aunt. I began to feel the train shudder. It began to rock about violently. I went to complain to the driver – no driver! I panicked. I began to press all the levers and suddenly the train toppled over altogether.

Lee Goodgame

Now begin to revise this narrative with your writing partner. Work together to try and make this a prizewinning mini-saga.

© Neil MacRae ISBN 1-85346-858-4

Activity 6

Mini-sagas 3 Pan for your own gold

Now it's time to write your own mini-saga.

Many of the mini-sagas you have now read work because they look at something in an unusual way or from a different point of view – the story of the Trojan Horse or the capture of a dolphin. Sometimes there is an unexpected twist at the end.

Here are three key tips to help you when writing your mini-saga.

> * Get a good idea. This is the most important start you can make. Look at some of the story ideas in Chapter 1. Brainstorm ideas based on situations. If these don't give you a starting point, discuss some of these structures with a partner. Can you work out some story ideas from real-life situations that can be shaped into a simple structure?

> * When you start, don't worry about the fifty-word limit to begin with. Concentrate on getting the narrative right. Then look at the words and phrases you can 'tighten up' so that every word counts.

> * Don't use the 'I woke up and it was all a dream' ending! This almost always makes the reader feel cheated.

© Neil MacRae ISBN 1-85346-858-4

3 The short short story

National Curriculum Framework links

Y7 – Writing

- plan, draft, edit, revise, proofread and present a text with readers and purpose in mind
- structure a story with an arresting opening, a developing plot, a complication, a crisis and satisfying resolution.

Y7 – Understanding the author's craft

- comment, using appropriate terminology, on how writers convey setting, character and mood through word choice and sentence structure
- recognise how writer's language choices can enhance meaning, e.g. repetition, emotive vocabulary, varied sentence structure or line length, sound effects
- trace the ways in which a writer structures a text to prepare a reader for the ending, and comment on the effectiveness of the ending.

Y8 – Writing

- experiment with different approaches to planning, drafting, proofreading and presenting writing, taking account of the time available
- re-read work to anticipate the effect on the reader and revise style and structure, as well as accuracy with this in mind.

Y8 – Understanding the author's craft

- analyse the overall structure of a text to identify how key ideas are developed, e.g. through the organisation of the content and the patterns of language used.

Pupil support

Gran's Last Journey is Kevin Crossley-Holland's retelling of a famous urban legend. Urban legends are the modern equivalent of those old legends that we find it difficult to believe in any more.

They have the same function as those old stories did: they are a reflection of the concerns we have about the world in which we live. An American professor, Jan Harald Brunvand, has spent years collecting these stories and identifying where they have come from. Some are over a hundred years old. They may also appear as the basis of poems, short stories, novels or films.

Brunvand tries to trace the history of this urban legend, which he calls *The Runaway Grandmother*. He has found that versions of this story appeared during the Second World War, when relatives were crossing international borders to escape persecution.

There is also a version of the story in John Steinbeck's novel *The Grapes of Wrath* (1939) in which Granma Joad's body is taken through the California agricultural inspection station (a kind of 'customs') wrapped in a blanket on the back of a truck. But Brunvand takes it even further back than that, linking it to a gruesome story popular in 15th-century Italy!

The table in Activity 3 can be enlarged to A3 (still in landscape format) for pupil completion. The results can be displayed around the classroom. The table could also be completed as an OHT, with the teacher modelling some of the key points of comparison and contrast.

To pupils, the writing of an urban legend may appear less demanding than being restricted by the imposed limitations of the mini-saga. This will prove illusory! The conventional narrative form will just appear more familiar to most pupils – they have written stories many times before and the danger is that this will lull them into a sense of false security.

Before pupils begin work on their own urban legend for Activity 6, it is important to set new challenges and demands. Teachers will need to gauge what will be appropriate here, but it is important that pupils have the structure of their narrative clear before they begin. The aim is to either use an existing story to create an individual narrative or to use a story model that is very tightly structured, with a clear understanding of plot, direction and the need for narrative and character limitations.

More able pupils should be encouraged to dig deeper into aspects of the conventions of the narrative. One that teachers can exploit at this point is the relationship between the writer and the reader. Crossley-Holland provides the reader with some verbal clues that suggest that this *will* indeed be Gran's final journey:

> 'But what I love most about travelling,' said Gran, 'is the way things never turn out quite as you expect.'

> 'The best holiday of all,' said Gran on their last evening. 'You know, I really could stay here for ever.'

Of course, the irony here is that it is Gran herself who provides this information.

The A4 copy of the story and the comparisons sheet provided in this chapter can both be used by pupils to note these and other features of the text. This should be followed by discussion about how this and other techniques observed can be used in pupils' own narratives.

Chapter 3 The short short story

Activity 1

Ready for more!

Need more words to develop your ideas? The short short story is usually just a few pages long, with the opportunity to develop the plot and the characters rather more than in the mini-saga.

The writer Kevin Crossley-Holland has written a collection of short short stories called *Short!* All the stories are less than two pages long – and one is just one sentence in length!

Read the example on the next page.

Write down your thoughts about this story. Were there clues about what was going to happen? Note ideas in the box below or in your workbook.

© Neil MacRae ISBN 1-85346-858-4

Activity 1 (continued)

Gran's Last Journey by Kevin Crossley-Holland

GRAN LOVED SWITZERLAND. She loved the little rackety mountain trains, the muesli and spit-and-polish, and the mountains with icing on them that turned pink in the evening sunlight.

'But what I love most about travelling,' said Gran, 'is the way things never turn out quite as you expect.'

Gran had been to a mountain village in Switzerland for her honeymoon and, ten years later, she somehow raised enough money to take her daughter there.

'How did you do that?' her daughter asked her, when she was grown up. 'Where did the money come from?'

'I sold my engagement ring,' said Gran.

'You didn't.'

'Dad agreed. One ring's enough for anybody.'

So when Gran was seventy-nine, there was a lot of talk around the kitchen table. And in the end, Gran's daughter and her husband and their two children decided to club together for Gran's eightieth birthday. They decided to drive across France and get Gran out to Switzerland one more time.

What a holiday they had! Picnics; walks through springy, sweet-smelling pinewoods; paddling through streams so icy cold the water grabbed your ankles; little expeditions up and down the village street; meals by candlelight.

'The best holiday of all,' said Gran on their last evening. 'You know, I really could stay here for ever.'

And that night, without any fuss, Gran died in her sleep. She just sighed, and let out all her breath, and didn't breathe in again.

'In this place of all places,' said her daughter, crying and smiling.

'Look! We don't want to get caught up with the authorities,' said her husband.' Gran would hate that. Let's just wrap her up and strap her to the roof-rack and get her home.'

And that's what the family decided to do. They packed their cases, wrapped up Gran, strapped her to the roof-rack, and all went back into the hotel for a late breakfast. In the dining-room, they stared at the high mountains and raised their mugs of steaming coffee. 'Adieu, Gran!' they said. 'Adieu!'

But when they came out of the hotel, blinking at the bright light, their car wasn't there. No car; no Gran; nothing.

'It's been stolen! Absolutely everything!'

Then they began to laugh.

'Gran would be laughing too,' her daughter said. 'She did love travelling.'

Activity 2

Introducing urban legends

Was the story about Gran's last journey familiar to you?

It is actually Kevin Crossley-Holland's retelling of a famous urban legend. Urban legends are the modern equivalent of those old legends that we find it difficult to believe in any more.

Here's how Kevin Crossley-Holland's story was summarised in a newspaper article over twenty years ago. Read the story carefully.

Where Did Granny Go?

A young couple about to get married cannot afford a honeymoon. Enter the granny. She has always wanted to see Spain. If they take her with them, she will pay for the honeymoon. She will be no trouble.

But during the honeymoon, in deepest Spain, she dies. Now they are really in a fix: the old lady has insisted in her will on cremation, and that is illegal in Spain. But the day before, the young couple had bought a carpet. At their wits' end, they decide to roll the old lady in it, put the body on the roof rack and make for France and the nearest crematorium.

Finally, they are over the border. They have passed safely through Customs. They stop the car and stagger into the nearest bar. When they come out, the car has been stolen. They never see it, the carpet, or granny ever again.

As with all urban legends, it is almost impossible to trace the origins of the story of the disappearing granny. These stories just seem to evolve over the years.

© Neil MacRae ISBN 1-85346-858-4

Activity 2 (continued)

Now read this oral version, told to Jan Harald Brunvand in his book *The Vanishing Hitchhiker.*

'This story was told to me by my cousin, who had heard it from a friend in Leeds, about a couple whom he knew, who went for a camping holiday in Spain with their car. They had taken their stepmother with them. She slept in a different tent to the others.

On the morning that they struck camp (to leave), they were busy and they didn't hear anything of her for a while, and then, when they went to her tent, they found she had died and rigor had already set in. They were in a great state, and they didn't know what to do, but they decided to roll her up in the tent, and put her on top of the car, and go to the nearest town, and go to the police.

So they did this ... and then they felt very cold and miserable, and they hadn't had a proper breakfast. So they thought they'd get a cup of coffee .... They parked the car and went to a small cafe and had their cup of coffee and then came back to look for the car. But it wasn't there. It had gone.

So they went home to England without the car or the stepmother.'

What has Crossley-Holland done with this urban legend? How has he used his writer's skills to make a straightforward telling of key events into a great short story? Note your ideas in the box below or in your workbook.

Activity 3

So where did Granny go?

Now you are ready to work with a partner on your response to this urban legend. Using the table provided, show the differences between the two reports and *Gran's Last Journey*.

Then use the final row in the table to identify some of the techniques used by Kevin Crossley-Holland to make his story more interesting for the reader.

	Report 1	*Report 2*	*Gran's Last Journey*
key facts			
people			
writer's techniques in Gran's Last Journey			

Now discuss in a group or as a whole class what you have noted about the three different versions. Look closely at the writer's techniques and especially how he signals what might happen. Note down some of the phrases he uses that show this.

© Neil MacRae ISBN 1-85346-858-4

Activity 4

Where you least expect them

Urban legends can come to us in different forms. Read this rather gruesome (but funny) poem:

Thank You, Dad, for Everything

Thank you for laying the carpet, Dad,
Thank you for showing us how,
But what is that lump in the middle, Dad?
And why is it saying miaow?

Doug MacLeod

Yes, this is an urban legend too! Discuss with your partner how this one might have developed and make some notes about your ideas.

Edward Lowbury's poem *Prince Kano* is also a story that has travelled around the world. Kano is a city in northern Nigeria so perhaps Lowbury came across the story in a version traditional in that country. Talk about the features of this urban legend and note down your ideas with your partner.

Prince Kano

In a dark wood Prince Kano lost his way
And searched in vain through the long summer's day.
At last, when night was near, he came in sight
Of a small clearing filled with yellow light,
And there, bending beside his brazier, stood
A charcoal burner wearing a black hood.
The Prince cried out for joy: 'Good friend, I'll give
What you will ask – guide me to where I live.'
The man pulled back his hood: he had no face –
Where it should be there was an empty space.

Half dead with fear the Prince staggered away,
Rushed blindly through the wood till break of day;
And then he saw a larger clearing filled
With houses, people: but his soul was chilled.
He looked around for comfort, and his search
Led him inside a small half-empty church
Where monks prayed. 'Father,' to one he said,
'I've seen a dreadful thing: I saw a man
Whose face was like . . .' and, as the Prince began,
The monk drew back his hood and seemed to hiss,
Pointing to where his face should be, 'Like this?'

Edward Lowbury

Activity 5

Over to you – writing your urban legend

Using urban legends as the starting point for your narratives can really work. You have the outline of a good story, you know what the ending might be and yet you have complete freedom to choose location, characters and how you tell the story.

For your main writing task in this chapter, you should create your own narrative from an urban legend. As most urban legends are told by word of mouth, this might be how your narrative will begin.

Before you begin your narrative, use the diagram below to help you start writing. Put the title of a legend in the circle and brainstorm some ideas about each of the key things you have learned so far, under the headings below.

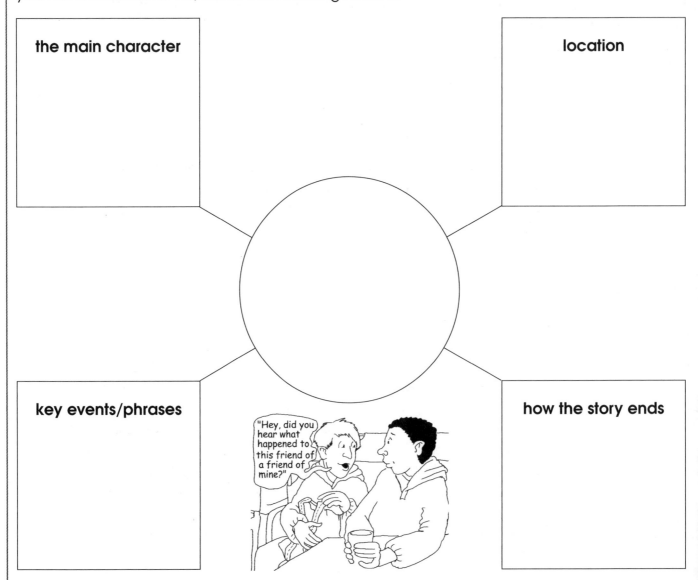

Two people meet up in a café, a pub or in the playground. As all urban legends are difficult to prove, the story should start with one person (who could be you) telling the other 'Hey, did you hear what happened to this friend of a friend of mine?' Use your own phrasing to get the tone of conversation right and then get into the story with another phrase like 'Well, it all started when . . .' This can be a great way to begin your urban legend.

© Neil MacRae ISBN 1-85346-858-4

Activity 5 (continued)

Michael Rosen uses this technique in his *Bakerloo Flea Woman* stories. This is how one of them begins. The two people meet on a bus...

I was on the last bus going down Willesden Lane one Wednesday night. I was going to stay with a friend that way. I was upstairs looking down on the street below when I heard this awful coughing. So I looked round and it was the Bakerloo Flea woman – the woman who knew all about those wasps, and all that.

'I don't believe it,' I said.

'Hello,' she said. 'Can't keep out of each other's way, can we? It's becoming a bit of a habit, isn't it?'

'Don't like your cough,' I said.

'Do you think I do?' she said.

'I suppose not,' I said.

'It's not as if it's the only thing I'm bothered by,' she said.

'Don't tell me,' I said. 'You've got a... er... a plague of something – slugs. Giant slugs in your bath.'

'Don't be funny,' she says.

'I'm sorry.'

She didn't say anything, so I asked her myself.

'Well, what's bothering you?' I said.

'Oh, it's only a little thing.'

'Yeah?' I said, not believing her.

'Well, I'm not superstitious,' she said. 'I don't believe in any of these things like horoscopes or fortune-telling. None of it.'

'Neither do I,' I said.

'But I used to have mice in my house.'

'Don't we all?' I said.

'I don't any more,' she said.

'Lucky you,' I said.

'Not a bit of it. I'd give anything in the world to have one or two of the little devils back, if I could.'

From *The Loaf and the Knife*, Michael Rosen

The rest of Rosen's story tells the horrific tale of why the Bakerloo Flea Woman wants the mice back and how there is a picture in her eye that 'can't be wiped out.'

You will come across this story again in a later Activity.

Only now are you ready to start writing! Use one of the urban legends you have read so far or work out a new narrative based on the key features of an urban legend. Make sure that you work out the ending of your narrative before you begin.

4 Getting characters right

Y8 – Writing

- *experiment with different approaches to planning, drafting, proofreading and presenting writing, taking account of the time available.*

Y8 – Understanding the author's craft

- *analyse the overall structure of a text to identify how key ideas are developed, e.g. through the organisation of the content and the patterns of language used*
- *investigate the different ways familiar themes are explored and presented by different writers.*

Y9 – Writing

- *review their ability to write for a range of purposes and audiences, recognising strengths and identifying skills for further development.*

Y9 – Understanding the author's craft

- *comment on interpretations of the same text or idea in different media, using terms appropriate for critical analysis.*

Pupil support

At the centre of this chapter is a key understanding about character in the narrative. Pupils will write better narratives if they understand that characters in a novel or short story (or film, television programme, joke or urban legend) have a function or purpose. In this they are, of course, different from people in real life. This is not always easy for pupils to take on board.

Most books about media texts will explore narrative theory. This classroom-centred text has already used the work of Genette to help distinguish between stories and narratives. This chapter goes further and uses the work of Russian theorist Vladimir Propp to help identify common structures in narratives. Propp's work is often used in film analysis, but it has an equal relevance for pupil narratives produced for Key Stage 3.

Propp's work *The Morphology of the Folk Tale* (1928) investigated hundreds of folk tales that fell into what he called the 'heroic wondertale' category. He noted a range of clearly identified common structures. Linking characters and their actions together, Propp identified eight different kinds of character and thirty-one different kinds of action. These actions or functions showed that characters did particular things at particular points in the story. For example, the villain – one of the eight characters – would always be punished at the end of the story.

Vladimir Propp character types

The villain – who will be punished at the end of the story.
The hero – or character who seeks something, but who won't necessarily be heroic.
The donor – who provides the hero with an object that that has some magic property(ies).
The helper – who aids the hero.
The sought-for person – who traditionally was usually a princess and the reward for the hero.
Her father – who consents to the reward.
The dispatcher – who sends the hero on his way.
The false hero – who may be unmasked as a villain.

There may be more than one person in a narrative with these character roles. Pupils should be encouraged to see how many of these characters they can recognise in fairy tales they remember. In Activity 3 they are asked to guess what some of the character types might be.

Teachers should develop this discussion and analysis into contemporary stories – particularly using films as the stimulus. The *Star Wars* films intentionally adopt this kind of structure and the recent interest in the 'sword and sorcery' genre through the *Harry Potter* novels and the *Lord of the Rings* films should encourage further debate.

It is important that the outcome of this is an understanding of the need to structure the narrative and give functionality to the characters – the plot needs order, and characters need a reason to be in the story.

It is easier to write about characters that have been seen or are based on people known to the writer. To write about a completely new character is more difficult. As a way into this and to begin the first step in a narrative featuring a new creation, pupils could play a version of Surrealist André Breton's game *Exquisite Corpses* – itself a version of the parlour game *Consequences*.

Each pupil uses a sheet of paper folded to allow four sections. These sections will finally contain a head, upper torso and arms, lower torso and hands, legs and feet, all joined together. After the head is drawn (with continuity marks to show where the next section must begin), pupils pass their now folded piece of paper on. When all sections are complete, the paper is returned to the original pupil who unfolds the paper to reveal a new character.

Pupils must then name their 'exquisite corpse' and then write down some descriptors – physical attributes, personal qualities, and so on. They should then provide three imagined likes and dislikes – ideally related to the developing portrait of the character. Finally, pupils should write down two sentences – one revealing an aspect of their character that they like and one an aspect they dislike.

Activity 4 uses a still from the opening of the film *Danny, Champion of the World*. If teachers are able to access the film itself and have a four-head video recorder that will allow a good freeze-frame facility, then some effective media literacy work can be used to develop pupil understanding of how the film narrative works.

This still gives a clear impression of Victor Hazell, the villain of the story. Hazell is a *nouveau riche* landowner whose ostentatious lifestyle is presented clearly with a short series of images at the start of the film – Hazell standing in front of his mansion, then Hazell driving his Rolls-Royce, looking down on the garage through his binoculars and so on. The clothes worn by Hazell – the bright yellow waistcoat, the tweedy plus-fours and so on – make it clear that his attitude to the countryside is similar to that of Toad in the *Wind in the Willows*. Hazell has bought into the country lifestyle but will forever be an outsider. If pupils are taken through this opening sequence, they will have a clearer idea of how film provides narrative information through a series of related visual images. Many films will be able to provide this insight.

Teachers may wish to extend this work with more able pupils through two further and contrasting refinements – using *Through the Keyhole* and the Sherlock Holmes short stories.

'So, David, who lives in a house like this?' was the question addressed by Lloyd Grossman to David Frost in a popular daytime television game. Lifestyle shows of this kind are all about character: here, contestants view film of Lloyd Grossman taking a camera crew through the home of a minor celebrity and are asked then to guess the name of the owner from a series of visual clues. These will all relate to the life and lifestyle of the celebrity and usually consist of a series of appropriate artefacts and props, all artfully placed to ensure maximum exposure.

This is little different from the personality-based sleuthing method applied by Sherlock Holmes to the procession of visitors that arrived at 221B Baker Street at the start of many investigations. The opening of *The Red-headed League* is a good example, and is used in Chapter 6.

Pupils have grown up with the concept of lifestyle – for one thing, it is the guiding principle behind the advertising they know and like. They have an implicit knowledge about characterisation from their reading of visual texts and their fascination with lifestyle and genre convention. Teachers can use this knowledge and begin to structure and codify it so that it can be used in their writing. One alternative starting point here would be a more detailed exploration of genre-based characterisation, using character stereotypes in science fiction, the western, the gothic and so on.

Chapter 4 Getting characters right

Activity 1

But who is in it?

So far in this book, we have focused on telling the story and looking at how and why narratives work. But there is something else that you will have included in your narratives already – *characters*.

If we were to ask most readers what makes a good story, the two key elements of

a good plot

and

characters that we can get involved with

would come up every time!

Think about characters in stories you have read and films you have seen. Discuss what makes an interesting character with your partner. Jot down some ideas in the box below or in your workbook.

© Neil MacRae ISBN 1-85346-858-4

Activity 2

What characters do

No matter how good the plot in a novel or short story might be, if we don't enjoy reading about the characters in the story we will not be entertained as much. The same is true of films and television programmes. You will probably have seen a film in which the action is exciting but the characters are poorly presented.

We like stories because of what characters *do*, not just who they are. This tells us something very important about the difference between people in real life and characters – in stories, films, television programmes, jokes – and urban legends. In our everyday lives we often find that things happen to us that are unplanned or unexpected. Even if we think our lives very boring, we can't say exactly what will happen to us from day to day!

But fictional characters are different from people in real life. They have been put in the book, film, television programme, joke or urban legend by the creator and for a purpose. This is a very important point to remember: it reminds us that the characters we put into a narrative (even if they are real or are based on real people) have a purpose or *function* and we need to use them in this way.

With a partner, think of five different main characters in stories, films or on television. Identify the key things they do in the narrative. Can you see any similarities in their roles? Don't be surprised if you can! Note down your ideas and discuss your conclusions.

Activity 3

From fairy tale to Star Wars

In the 1920s a Russian writer, Vladimir Propp, looked at hundreds of examples of one kind of story – the folk tale. He wanted to see whether they shared common structures, and he discovered that they did.

He linked characters and their actions together, identifying eight different kinds of character and thirty-one different kinds of action. These actions or functions showed that characters did particular things at particular points in the story. For example, the villain – one of the eight characters – would always be punished at the end of the story.

Can you guess what some of the other seven character types were? To help you begin, start with the opposite of the villain, and then think about the rôles or jobs that different characters have in the folk and fairy tales you have read or heard about when you were younger. Discuss with a partner what the seven characters might be and then ask your teacher and see if you are right! Now, can you make links between fairy tales you know and more modern stories you have read or films you have seen?

© Neil MacRae ISBN 1-85346-858-4

Activity 4

Writing about characters, 1

There are two ways to write about characters. To show the differences between these two approaches, try this activity:

Look at the character below in a scene from a film.

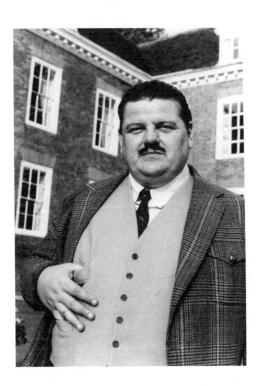

1   In your workbooks or in the box below, write down three sentences that tell us about what this character looks like. Describe how he relates to the house in the background.

2   How do you *think* he might have got to where he is now? Again, write down three sentences that might describe key moments in the life of this character.

Compare what you have written with others. Why did you make the links between character, house and background that you did?

This way of describing a character *tells* us about them – from the way they dress and behave to what they feel and believe. We can also find out about a character through what the writer *shows* us about what they think or feel.

Activity 5

Writing about characters, 2

Imagine the character shown in Activity 4 in the film, *Danny, the Champion of the World*. How would the film show this character walking out of the house and standing in front of the entrance? Imagine that you are providing directions to the actor in the film about the way to move to show the kind of person he is playing.

Think of what you would say and then, in the box below or in your workbook, write down three sentences that show the character's personality rather than what they look like.

Now, take this one step further and imagine that the same character is describing this photograph of himself – what would he say about it in his own words?

Again, write three sentences – but put them in speech marks as if the character was talking about himself. What does this show us about the character?

Here, the character is literally *speaking* for himself – but do we trust what he says? Characters might not always tell the truth.

Activity 6

Bringing it all together

Writers use each of these three approaches when they describe characters. Try it yourself by expanding on a very basic starter sentence, the kind of sentence you remember from when you first learned to read. Here are three examples:

> James ate his breakfast.

> Chris looked out of the window.

> Aisha walked down the lane.

When writing about characters, a balance between these different approaches (**telling**, **showing**, **dialogue**) really works. Have a look at the example below, created using one of the sentence starters.

> James slowly dipped the spoon into his soggy cornflakes. 'Games!' he muttered and shook his head. 'No way.' Then, and loudly enough for his mum to hear, he groaned and put his head on the kitchen table. 'Mum,' he cried, 'I don't feel well.'

What does this reveal about James? Can you see where the three different approaches to writing about character have been used?

Now, using each of the three starter sentences above, expand them by using four or five new sentences that use some or all of these approaches. Think carefully about the characters you are creating. Try to make your *James ate his breakfast* sentences as different as possible from the example above! Write your three openings in your workbooks or in the boxes on the next sheet.

Activity 6 (continued)

Now share the completed character descriptions with a partner. Look closely at the descriptions that have been created. Try to identify the different kinds of writing about character that your partner has used. Can you imagine these characters?

Do any of the descriptions give you ideas for a narrative in which one or more of the characters might appear? If so, note down any details about the narrative and think about how they might be used later.

It is important to be aware of this mix of different kinds of description whenever you are writing narratives.

These character portraits might make good display material – and ideas for others too!

© Neil MacRae ISBN 1-85346-858-4

Activity 7

The Vanishing Hitchhiker 1

We learn about characters in narratives from what the writer says about them. But we often get as much information from what they say too. In most stories, writers use the dialogue between characters as a way to tell us about them *and* to move the story on.

Just as the characters and their actions have functions in the narrative, so does the dialogue. Dialogue isn't always like real-life conversation. If we were to tape-record the conversations we have with friends, it wouldn't always make good reading! Most of the time when we talk we don't think about how it might relate to things we will say later on. In narratives, we need to make sure that what characters say is related to the ideas in the story.

Remember the urban legend? Well, here is one of the most famous of all urban legends – the vanishing hitchhiker.

A taxi driver is driving home late at night to Birkenhead.[1] As he nears the entrance to the Mersey Tunnel he sees a hitchhiker and stops to give the figure a lift. The hiker is a girl and, seeing her shiver, the driver lends her a sweater. She tells him her address in Birkenhead but then, as they emerge from the Tunnel, he turns and the girl is just not there.

In great bewilderment he calls at the address. An elderly woman answers the door and he tells her his tale. As he does so, he notices that she is crying. She goes back into the house and returns with a photo of a girl – the hiker. She explains that it is her daughter who was killed in a car accident in the Mersey Tunnel. The man does not believe her but the woman tells him the address of the cemetery where the girl has been buried.

Curious, the taxi driver goes to the cemetery and walks among the graves until he sees one with a sweater draped over it. It is his sweater. He bends down to read the writing on the grave and it is the girl's grave.

---

[1] The Mersey Tunnel links the city of Liverpool on the northern side of the river with the town of Birkenhead on the southern side.

Activity 7 (continued)

As before, this outline of the story is just a starting point. This time, you are going to work on developing the three characters so that the narrative is moved forward by what they reveal to us.

First, we need to look closely at the story outline. You might have heard versions of this story before. If you have, share these first – and note the differences.

Now – discuss this key question:

> The girl is a ghost – how can this be developed in the story?

Talk to a partner about how you might do this. Think carefully about the information you have learned already in this chapter. Note down your ideas in the box.

© Neil MacRae ISBN 1-85346-858-4

Activity 8

The Vanishing Hitchhiker 2

Now read the narrative extract below:

> Rain threw itself onto Roy's windscreen. The taxi's wiper blades struggled to clear the screen and Roy quickly brushed his coat cuff against the inside of the glass. 'Thank God,' he thought. 'That's me finished for the day.' Ahead of him were the narrow lanes leading to the entrance to the Mersey Tunnel and, beyond that, home in Birkenhead. Roy shivered.

Compare this with the same section from the original story outline:

> A taxi driver is driving home late at night to Birkenhead. As he nears the entrance to the Mersey Tunnel . . .

What has the narration added? There is much more detail about the setting of the story, but we also know much more about the driver. Think about telling, showing and dialogue.

What can you say about the character of the driver now? In the box below or in your workbook note down some ideas.

Activity 9

The Vanishing Hitchhiker 3

Now read the next section of the story outline. *We* now know that the girl is a ghost – but the new reader does not! How could a clue be included in a narrative version of this outline?

Write your expansion of this next section of the story:

> . . . he sees a hitchhiker and stops to give the figure a lift. The hiker is a girl and, seeing her shiver, the driver lends her a sweater. She tells him her address in Birkenhead, but then, as they emerge from the Tunnel, he turns and the girl is just not there.

Remember to use a mix of telling, showing and dialogue and don't forget – the hitchhiker is a ghost!

© Neil MacRae ISBN 1-85346-858-4

Activity 10

Your *Vanishing Hitchhiker* narrative

Like all urban legends, *The Vanishing Hitchhiker* has a strong plot, but what really makes a good narrative from this basic story outline is the quality of the characters. We have contrasts between the kind driver, the lost girl ghost and the grieving mother.

You now have to make these characters come alive (even the ghost!) and help to move the story forward. You should create a longer narrative than before and develop the characters, using the three techniques of telling, showing and character dialogue.

Six top tips:

- Think about when you will use each technique.
- Think about the effects you want to achieve.
- Remember that the outline of the story gives you all the plot you need.
- Don't add more characters or scenes.
- Concentrate on making the reader want to read on.
- Remember that you know the story – but for your reader it is all new!

This time, when you complete your narrative, try and test it on a friend by reading it aloud to them.

© Neil MacRae ISBN 1-85346-858-4

5 Graphic ideas

National Curriculum Framework links

Y8 – Writing

- *experiment with different approaches to planning, drafting, proofreading and presenting writing, taking account of the time available.*

Y8 – Understanding the author's craft

- *analyse the overall structure of a text to identify how key ideas are developed, e.g. through the organisation of the content and the patterns of language used*
- *investigate the different ways familiar themes are explored and presented by different writers.*

Y9 – Writing

- *review pupils' ability to write for a range of purposes and audiences, recognising strengths and identifying skills for further development.*

Y9 – Understanding the author's craft

- *comment on interpretations of the same text or idea in different media, using terms appropriate for critical analysis.*

Pupil support

To support Activity 2 and develop these ideas further, pupils could look for other photographs that could start or end a narrative. They will not need to be as dramatic as the one provided. Newspaper articles and advertisements are rich sources of good photo ideas. Pupils will have noticed that advertisements in magazines and on television are often little narratives.

Activity 6 requires pupils to look at a range of television advertisements. The teacher should guide pupils to focus on advertisements that have strong characters embedded in a narrative. Most 'lifestyle' advertisements will have this approach. Some specific types of advertisement are indicated below:

- food advertisements that deal with families (e.g. advertisements for spaghetti sauces or olive oil-based spreads);
- supermarket advertisements that focus on members of a family (e.g. the *Tesco* advertisements that featured Prunella Scales and her 'daughter' Jane Horrocks);
- car advertisements that are about relationships (e.g. the advertisements for the Ford Focus and Fiat Punto or the series of advertisements for Peugeot cars).

There are a number of collections of suitable advertisements that could be successfully used. Teachers may wish to videotape a selection of current choices or ask pupils to view their own choices.

Activity 1

New ideas for narratives

Ideas for narratives can come from all kinds of sources. Ask any writer! It's not that writers lead much more exciting lives than the rest of us – but what they *are* good at is storing ideas to use later on.

Ideas don't have to come from things that happen to us directly. Writers take theirs from all kinds of sources and this chapter is about using just one of those sources – the things we see around us.

Think of what has happened to you over the last week. Focus on remembering one powerful image – it could be your choice of school dinner, something seen on the television news, the clothes worn by someone in the street . . .

Jot down a description of what you remember seeing, in the box below or in your workbook.

Any of these images might be enough to start an idea for a story. What writers often do is put together a series of images.

If we are to develop a narrative from visual sources, we will need to look at a range of different kinds of images. Some will help us with the *plot*, some with the *characters* and some with the *atmosphere* we want to create. This chapter explores how each of these areas of a narrative can be developed and, at the end of the chapter, you will pull together your ideas in preparation for using them in a final activity in the next chapter.

Activity 2

Reading pictures – the photostory

It is said that a picture is worth a thousand words. Photojournalists tell stories through pictures. Look at this award-winning press photo.

The woman and the girl were waiting for rescue from a burning building. Tragically, the woman died but the child survived.

In the box below or in your workbook, jot down some notes to structure a narrative that would build up to this final scene. Share your notes with others and build up a range of plot ideas. These might provide you with some good starting points for a story.

Stanley Forman

© Neil MacRae ISBN 1-85346-858-4

Activity 3

From pictures to story

Many advertisements have become famous because they tell stories. A series of advertisements for the stockcube *Oxo* showed a 'typical' family growing up, sitting around the dinner table and so on, and a celebrated series for *Gold Blend* coffee made the couple who featured in the advertisements into stars. If you have been to the cinema recently, you will know those long cinema advertisements that are more like short films. Think about some you have seen recently and discuss with a partner the stories they tell.

For this activity, you will need to collect advertisements and photographs. Select two of the images – one to be the start of your narrative and one the end. If possible, present the two images at either end of a large sheet of paper. At least one of the images should have a figure that can be presented as the central character in your narrative.

Now, between the two images – and working on your own – write the **outline** (but not the narrative itself) that links them. It doesn't matter if your narrative is unusual or strange – this is quite likely! Focus on developing some key aspects of the plot, characters and atmosphere but don't make your narrative too complex. Keep it simple.

Compare your ideas with others. Discuss in larger groups and identify the features of any narratives that make them work. If possible, create a display of some of the image narratives.

Using the collection of images, note down all the ideas for narratives that you have so far. Remember that you may be using one or more of these ideas in the narrative that you will create at the end of this chapter.

Activity 4

It's cartoon time!

Cartoons aren't easy! In a small space, the artist/writer has to tell a story using an interesting character. Because there isn't much time or space to develop character, cartoons often feature stereotypes. Think of favourite characters from cartoon strips you read when you were younger. Usually, the names were enough to tell you what the character was like!

Most cartoon strips are driven by *plot*: the character behaves in the way we expect in response to different situations each week. This is very useful – we can pick up ideas for narratives from the typical plots found in cartoons.

Work out the structure of 'A Day in the Life of Arnie' (on the next page) by summarising what happens. Write your summary in the first five boxes below. Think carefully about how the narrative has been put together. The first events of the narrative have been completed for you in the first box.

The last box here is for you to summarise what will happen in the final few missing frames. Does the narrative so far reveal a structure that you have met in other cartoon strips? You might be reminded of other famous animated cartoon animals that have long-running battles!

Study other cartoon strips – in magazines, newspapers or comics. Summarise some of their plots that could be used in a written narrative. Are any of them common to different cartoons? Try and represent them as a diagram or flow chart that shows how the plot works.

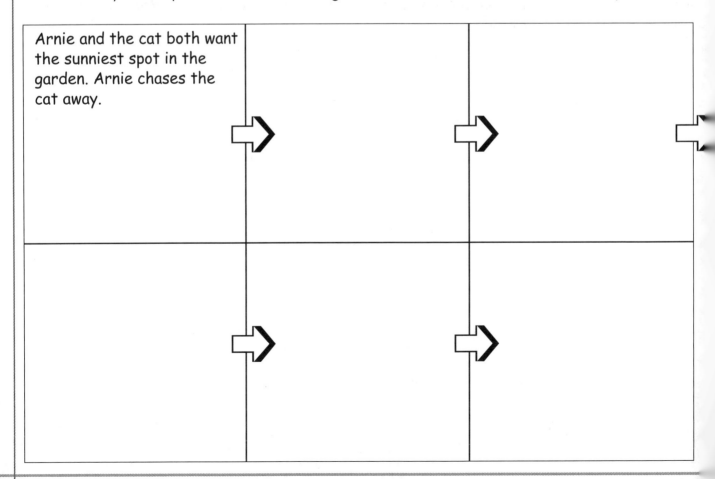

Arnie and the cat both want the sunniest spot in the garden. Arnie chases the cat away.

© Neil MacRae ISBN 1-85346-858-4

Activity 4 (continued)

'A Day in the Life of Arnie' – by Michelle Gale and Bryan Hitch

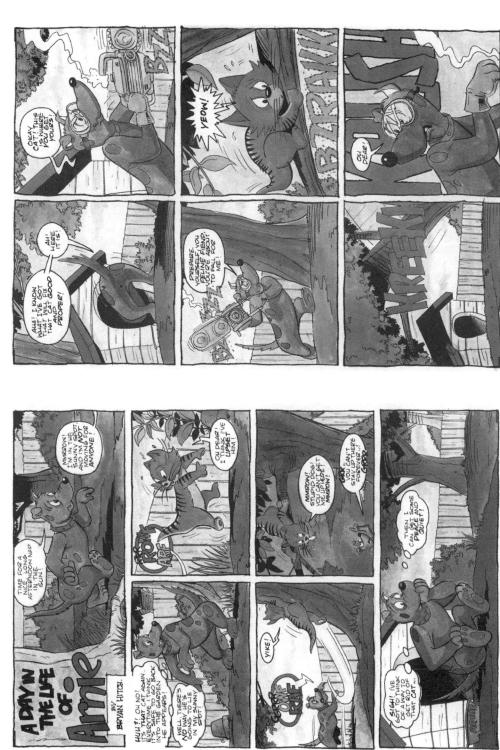

Look closely at the first twelve frames of this cartoon. How do you think it will end?

'A Day in the Life of Arnie', idea by school pupil Michelle Gale, drawn by Bryan Hitch, published in Cartoon Kidz 1989. Cartoon Aid Ltd, Business Design Centre, 52 Upper Street, Islington, London.

Activity 5

Fashion victim

Images can be just as helpful when we need to develop *characters* for our narratives.

What we wear usually says something about us – even if we don't want it to! Look at the photographs on this page and begin to create a character from one of the images.

To help you, answer these questions about your character:

- What is this person's favourite item of clothing and why?

- Describe the kind of house in which this person would like to live.

- What sort of music does this person listen to?

- What would be the job they would most like to have?

- If this person was given an air ticket to anywhere, where would they fly to?

- What do you most like and dislike about this person?

- Now – give the character you have created an appropriate name.

Activity 6

Seen on screen

Television advertisements have to work hard. In 50 seconds or less they need to make us think about a product. Sometimes this will be done through the creation of a strong character.

Watch some current television advertisements. Focus on advertisements that feature characters in a narrative setting. You will find that many advertisements do – from spaghetti sauces to cars!

Remember to look *closely* at these advertisements. Some of them will have tiny details that you won't notice from just one viewing. If you have an opportunity to use a freeze-frame facility, then this will help.

To help you, use this grid to write down your thoughts on the advertisements you watch.

Seen on screen – characters in advertisements	
Summary of the advertisement What happens in the ad? Describe the main events and the style and the setting	
Character description **Explicit:** what the character is wearing, the way he/she moves, talks, etc.	
Character description **Implicit:** how the character relates to those around him/her, how the camera shows the character – angles, close-up/long shot, etc.	

Share some of the ideas for characters you have developed from your work in this chapter. Remember that you may be using some of these ideas in the narrative that you will create at the end of this chapter.

Activity 7

'Of course, in my day... blah, blah, blah...'

> 'Of course, in my day, the summer holidays were much longer and the weather was better too. Yes, I must have been about your age and I can remember walking along the front at Whittling-by-the-Sea with a huge portion of chips in my hand. Sixpence they cost - and a huge bag it was too. Not like the little french fries you get these days...'

I'm sure you have heard conversations a bit like this! It's the little atmospheric details that we remember (or *think* we remember) from our childhood that become important memories later on.

Take a memory from your own childhood now – perhaps a place you visited, something you ate, a relative you remember – and write a brief but exaggerated description of the memory. Think carefully about significant details and write no more than 150 words.

Activity 8

Atmospherics

The third way in which images can help a writer is by generating atmosphere – a sense of feeling or presence. Think about how advertisers or film- and videomakers choose black and white images to create a particular feeling.

Take a look at this photograph.

In your workbook or using the box below, jot down some personal responses to the questions below and then compare your ideas with those of a partner.

- What is the first detail that you noticed?

- What colours or tones can you can see?

- Describe the weather in the photo.

- Describe the mood or atmosphere of the photo to someone else – what words would you use?

- Does the photo remind you of an object, a place or a person you know?

Now, build up a bank of words and phrases that sum up the photo. Locate these around the photo and display the results. Compare your annotated photos with those of others. Pick up ideas from the photos on display!

Activity 9

Putting it all together

You have now looked at a wide range of different sources of images and are ready for the final activity. Gather together all the ideas about plot, character and atmosphere from the previous activities in this chapter. Discuss each of these in a small group so that you are collecting more ideas for narratives. Think about how some of them may work together and note down ideas in the box below or in your workbook. Discuss the links you make with the whole group.

Remember, you are not going to write a story, but the ideas you gather may become part of your final story in the next chapter.

© Neil MacRae ISBN 1-85346-858-4

6 Superplots, timeshifting and problem-solving

National Curriculum Framework links

Y8 – Writing

- *experiment with different approaches to planning, drafting, proofreading and presenting writing, taking account of the time available.*

Y8 – Understanding the author's craft

- *analyse the overall structure of a text to identify how key ideas are developed, e.g. through the organisation of the content and the patterns of language used*
- *investigate the different ways familiar themes are explored and presented by different writers.*

Y9 – Writing

- *review the pupils' ability to write for a range of purposes and audiences, recognising strengths and identifying skills for further development.*

Y9 – Understanding the author's craft

- *comment on interpretations of the same text or idea in different media, using terms appropriate for critical analysis.*

Pupil support

As in Chapter 1, this unit focuses on plot. By this stage in their work, pupils should be more confident that they can produce better plot structures. At this point, it is useful to explore in more detail where plot structuring can go wrong for many pupils. There are two key reasons for this.

First, ideas may have come from incidents or events that have happened to the pupil writer – they are real and open-ended rather than structured into a narrative. This is often as a result of pupils believing that originality in a narrative comes through using events that are derived from their own experience. More important for young

writers is the ability to craft a story. This book focuses on craft techniques – and the message should continue to be endorsed in this final chapter.

Second, as Activity 7 explores, the narratives devised by young writers may be derived from film or television stories. As a result, and especially if written by boys, they are likely to rely on dialogue and sound effects. Alternatively, they may be so heavily plot driven that the James Bond-style car chase across five continents is delivered in 400 words!

The visual elements in these narratives are assumed by the writer to be in the head of the reader as they read – even if they haven't seen the film or television source. There may be an understanding of character and action, but it is linked to a visual, filmic presentation. The action is being 'run' as a film clip through the writer's head with the result that only the soundtrack emerges on the page. This is why such writers will include an account of noises ('beep, beep, beep') but not movement or action – this is implied only. This kind of writing is often characteristic of boys.

Activities 4 and 5 make reference to Roald Dahl's story *The Landlady*. Teachers might encourage pupils to read this (and other stories) and identify the techniques that Dahl uses.

In Activity 6, pupils might be able to better understand how the conversational delay used by some writers can be so effective if they can see or hear how comedians use this approach. The 'chair' monologues that were a Ronnie Corbett feature in the long-running television series *The Two Ronnies* well showed how the punchline moment is continually put off through a series of irrelevant digressions.

In preparation for Activity 10 – the final and most demanding piece of writing that pupils will undertake – teachers should again beware of the tyranny of the continuous prose draft. To have text 'set in stone' in this way can make it difficult to see where modification can be made. Teachers marking such material may not be able to offer much guidance beyond the technical. Getting the right structure first will be helpful for pupils.

Notes and drafts are best in a format suited to the final structure and teachers may find it useful (especially for less confident writers) to provide some kind of visual or diagrammatic structure to support the completion of the narrative.

One way to develop this would be through a flow-chart approach to planning the narrative. Pupils could be encouraged to develop supporting frames that suit their level of confidence (and competence) with narrative structure. One starting point can be the use of the term **CAD** – **C**haracter, **A**ction and **D**escription.

A flow chart that balances these three components would be a useful framing device for pupils. A simple version (which can be enlarged to A3 size) is provided at the end of Activity 10.

Pupils should use this before beginning their narrative. The central column of the plot (action) should be completed first and then character and descriptive elements can be added to support the plot. The arrows indicate how the Characters and Descriptions can be 'injected' into the Action (the plot). More confident writers will indicate where they will be using some of the devices covered in this final chapter.

Visualising the narrative in this way is a very effective way to tightly control the structure. Teachers may wish to be more prescriptive and provide clear models that support the needs of their particular pupils.

Activity 1

'As the walls began to close in, Chris suddenly remembered how it had all started...'

The Activities in this final chapter will do two things to help your writing. Some will give you ideas about how to include in your own writing some of the advanced techniques that writers use. Others include some ideas for solving some common problems in your writing. Finally, you will write a detective fiction narrative that will incorporate many of the ideas you have worked on in the Activities of the six chapters of *How to Teach Fiction Writing at Key Stage 3*.

To start with, here's a sure-fire way to make your narrative immediately more sophisticated. It is likely that most of the narratives you have written for the first five chapters of this book are chronological – the events in the story are told in the order in which they happen. But not all narratives work this way. Think either of a film you have seen or a story you have read in which the chronological order of events is changed. Perhaps the beginning of the film or narrative shows events that you later discover are at the end of the story.

Discuss this with a partner. Share the ideas about such narratives in your group.

Activity 2

Flashback

Many writers have used this non-chronological technique. It is often called *flashback*. The opening of S.E. Hinton's novel *The Outsiders* begins with the storyteller, Ponyboy. He is writing as an English essay the events that we are told about later in the novel. That opening line from *Rebecca* in Chapter 2 (*Last night I dreamt I went to Manderley again*) is another non-chronological start to a novel.

So why should a writer put the ending of a story at the beginning? Doesn't this 'give away' what happens? That will depend on how much the writer wants to reveal at this stage. Sometimes putting part of the ending of a narrative at the beginning can create real tension. The reader is teased by the writer and wants to find out more.

How does flashback work and how can you incorporate it into your narratives?

Start by thinking about the beginning and the ending of one of the narratives you have written already. Imagine taking the last section of a narrative and placing it at the beginning . . .

Look back at your workbook and find a narrative where this might be possible. Focus on no more than the last 150 words and imagine a new version of your narrative in which your ending is placed at the beginning of the story. Is this possible? How does the writing have to change?

Read the new opening of your narrative to a partner. Discuss your thoughts.

Activity 3

The Hitchhiker – vanished! 1

Think back to the summary of that urban legend *The Vanishing Hitchhiker* in Chapter 4, Activity 7. Let's take the last three-sentence paragraph and just put it at the beginning of the summary:

Curious, the taxi driver goes to the cemetery and walks among the graves until he sees one with a sweater draped over it. It is his sweater. He bends down to read the writing on the grave and it is the girl's grave.

A taxi driver is driving home late at night to Birkenhead. As he nears the entrance to the Mersey Tunnel he sees a hitchhiker and stops to give the figure a lift. The hiker is a girl and, seeing her shiver, the driver lends her a sweater. She tells him her address in Birkenhead, but then, as they emerge from the Tunnel, he turns and the girl is just not there.

In great bewilderment he calls at the address. An elderly woman answers the door and he tells her his tale. As he does so, he notices that she is crying. She goes back into the house and returns with a photo of a girl – the hiker. She explains that it is her daughter who was killed in a car accident in the Mersey Tunnel. The man does not believe her but the woman tells him the address of the cemetery where the girl has been buried.

Imagine the story *beginning* like this:

Roy walked among the gravestones. 'In memory of . . .'; 'My dearest husband . . .'; 'Forever in our thoughts . . .'. He hardly dared to look more closely at the inscriptions all around him. Then suddenly Roy stopped, his blood frozen. Surely, it couldn't be!

In front of him was a gravestone and on it was a sweater. His sweater. Slowly, Roy walked up to the stone and looked down to read the inscription . . .

Think of this opening scene as the start of a film. As Roy bends down to read the inscription, there is a cut. The next scene opens with Roy at the wheel of his taxi, peering through the rain-smeared windscreen as he drives towards the entrance to the Mersey Tunnel.

There is a clear change of chronology here, isn't there? If the viewer hadn't guessed that the next scene will now go back to an earlier moment in the story then the director could have made it a little more obvious.

Activity 3 (continued)

Close up on sweater draped over gravestone - thin layer of frost/dew on sweater.

Close up on Roy's face - blank horror.

Close up on Roy's feet - walking through wet grass towards gravestone.

Cut to gravestone and zoom/close up to inscription:

'In Memory of Our Dear Daughter

A Life Cut Short

Sarah Jane

4th February 1985 - 18th March 1999'

Close up on Roy's face - reaction. Roy stares into the distance.

Now, write your version of this extract from the film script as the opening of a narrative. Use the box below or write in your workbook.

© Neil MacRae ISBN 1-85346-858-4

Activity 4

'She seemed terribly nice...'

If a puppet show is good, you should be able to forget that there is a puppeteer controlling everything. It's the same with reading: the best writers will make you forget that they are controlling everything you read – and most of what you think!

Writers like to tease their readers. Sometimes they will plant *clues* about what is going to happen next. If the reader thinks that they have rather cleverly picked up these embedded clues, *they* feel in control! But the writer will have planned this too. One good way to do this is to make sure that your main character is an innocent, not fully aware of what is happening to him or her.

Horror films use this technique all the time. 'Don't go up those creaking stairs to that locked door,' we want to shout. But, of course, the naïve leading character always does! Writers use the same tricks – but how do they show this in words?

A quick way is to use the words 'seemed' or 'appeared'. In a thriller, horror or detective story, 'seemed' is often used like this:

> She seemed terribly nice. She looked exactly like the mother of one's best school-friend welcoming one into the house to stay for the Christmas holidays.
>
> From Roald Dahl, *The Landlady*

> The climb seemed easy enough. Nick had made similar ascents before. 'What could go wrong this time?' he thought.

Think of some scenes from typical thriller, horror or detective stories. Discuss these with a writing partner. Now, working together, take some of these scenes and write three short paragraph extracts from three different narratives that include the words 'seemed' or 'appeared' in this way.

Activity 5

The Hitchhiker – vanished! 2

In *The Landlady*, Roald Dahl makes sure that he gives us enough clues by the end of the story to have worked out what is happening to the main character, Billy Weaver. Unfortunately, Billy is still unaware of what has happened to him and the inevitable end to the story is – well, you will just have to read it yourself!

Writing a narrative with both a flashback and some embedded clues can help to achieve this effect successfully. Your next writing activity in this chapter is to write a new beginning to *The Vanishing Hitchhiker* using both these techniques. You should write only the section covered by the summary below:

Curious, the taxi driver goes to the cemetery and walks among the graves until he sees one with a sweater draped over it. It is his sweater. He bends down to read the writing on the grave and it is the girl's grave . . .

    The driver is driving home late at night to Birkenhead. As he nears the entrance to the Mersey Tunnel he sees a hitchhiker and stops to give the figure a lift. The hiker is a girl and, seeing her shiver, the driver lends her a sweater. She tells him her address in Birkenhead, but then, as they emerge from the Tunnel, he turns and the girl is just not there.

You can use some of your earlier story in this retelling – think of it as a first draft and focus on using these two new techniques. You must provide some clues that the girl is in fact a *ghost*. Don't tell the reader, but decide how easy you want to make it for them. Think about the most subtle ways that you could do this.

You should write no more than 400 words. When you have completed your retelling of this first section, share your work with a partner. Compare the ways in which you have developed these new techniques.

© Neil MacRae ISBN 1-85346-858-4

Activity 6

The Loaf and the Knife

Here are two final techniques that can be included in your writing. If you have listened to a joke being told by an expert, you will know that delaying the delivery of the punchline is a great way to keep us entertained.

Delay can also keep us in suspense. We have seen this at work already in Chapter 3 in a short extract from Michael Rosen's *The Loaf and the Knife*. Here Rosen uses conversation to delay the real start of the story. The Bakerloo Flea Woman is reluctant to reveal the details of the story, and the incidental details of the conversation keep us reading on. This technique is more difficult to do than it looks. Read the extract from the below.

Then look at the extract again and, with a highlighter pen, note all the dialogue that has nothing to do with the plot (which is about how the Bakerloo Flea Woman got rid of her mice) but is there only to delay the real start of the story. One example would be the mention of her cough!

So I looked round and it was the Bakerloo Flea woman – the woman who knew all about those wasps, and all that.

'I don't believe it,' I said.

'Hello,' she said. 'Can't keep out of each other's way, can we? It's becoming a bit of a habit, isn't it?'

'Don't like your cough,' I said.

'Do you think I do?' she said.

'I suppose not,' I said.

'It's not as if it's the only thing I'm bothered by,' she said.

'Don't tell me,' I said. 'You've got a . . . er . . . a plague of something – slugs. Giant slugs in your bath.'

'Don't be funny,' she says.

'I'm sorry.'

She didn't say anything, so I asked her myself.

'Well, what's bothering you?' I said.

'Oh, it's only a little thing.'

'Yeah?' I said, not believing her.

'Well, I'm not superstitious,' she said. 'I don't believe in any of these things like horoscopes or fortune-telling. None of it.'

'Neither do I,' I said.

'But I used to have mice in my house.'

'Don't we all?' I said.

'I don't any more,' she said.

'Lucky you,' I said.

'Not a bit of it. I'd give anything in the world to have one or two of the little devils back, if I could.'

From *The Loaf and the Knife*, Michael Rosen

Activity 7

Crash! Ring, ring!

Have you ever written dialogue like this?

> 'Beep, beep, beep, beep, beep!'
>
> 'Get down those stairs! You're late!'
>
> 'Argh!' thought Dave, 'I hate Mondays!'

Does this happen in your writing? Suddenly, without warning, a sound effect appears? The story is being run through your head, but only the sounds are being picked up and described. There is little detail in the description.

This kind of writing will include an account of noises ('beep, beep, beep') but have very little movement or action. This is implied only. Look at how a good writer conveys sound without sound effects but with some very powerful description. In doing so, the whole passage comes alive:

> The jungle was wide and full of twitterings, rustlings, murmurs and sighs.
> Suddenly it all ceased, as if someone had shut a door.
> Silence.
> A sound of thunder.
> Out of the mist, one hundred yards away, came *Tyrannosaurus Rex*.
> 'Jesus God,' whispered Eckels.
> 'Sh!'
> It came on great oiled, resilient, striding legs. It towered thirty feet above half of the trees, a great evil god, folding its delicate watchmaker's claws close to its oily reptilian chest. Each lower leg was a piston, a thousand pounds of white bone, sunk in thick ropes of muscle, sheathed over in a gleam of pebbled skin like the mail of a terrible warrior. Each thigh was a ton of meat, ivory and steel mesh. And from the great breathing cage of the upper body those two delicate arms dangled out front, arms with hands which might pick up and examine men like toys, while the snake neck coiled. And the head itself, a ton of sculptured stone, lifted easily upon the sky. Its mouth gaped, exposing a fence of teeth like daggers. Its eyes rolled, ostrich eggs, empty of all expression save hunger. It closed its mouth in a death grin. It ran, its pelvic bones crushing aside trees and bushes, its taloned feet clawing damp earth, leaving prints six inches deep wherever it settled its weight. It ran with a gliding ballet step, far too poised and balanced for its ten tons. It moved into a sunlit arena warily, its beautiful reptile hands feeling the air.
>
> From *A Sound of Thunder*, Ray Bradbury

Activity 7 (continued)

Discuss with a partner how this writer makes sound believable.

Note down some examples and share them with others.

Activity 8

'Don't open that door…'

In these narrative genres, a writer will often try and make sure that the reader feels they are one step ahead of the character and that they have picked up the clues – even if the character hasn't! This is often because the central character is the innocent victim in this kind of narrative. Horror films and thrillers work in the same way.

One way to represent this is shown below:

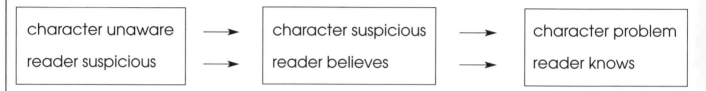

The order is usually the same: the writer or film director knows everything, and the reader or viewer is just one step ahead of the central character. For real shock value, of course, sometimes the writer or director will make sure that there is a point where there are no clues, and reader or viewer has a real shock!

Another way to show this movement across the narrative is like this:

character is suspicious ⟶ a revelation ⟶ more suspicions ⟶ another revelation ⟶ more suspicions ⟶ a final revelation.

The reader is teased along with a series of revelations about what is happening. Discuss with a partner examples of this technique that you have read in stories or seen on screen. Note down some examples and share them with others.

© Neil MacRae ISBN 1-85346-858-4

Activity 8 (continued)

This technique is often used in the genre that you are now going to use in your final piece of writing. Detective fiction is a genre that has been with us for a long time – nearly 200 years. We can trace this kind of writing back to the memoirs of a famous French policeman, Eugene Vidocq. Originally a criminal, while in prison he became a police informer. He was so successful that in 1811 he was given his freedom and appointed the first Chef de la Sûreté – the French detective force! At the end of his career and after many scandals he turned to writing. Always on the borderline between hero and villain, his character became the model for many later writers.

So where did the English detective, Sherlock Holmes, come from? His creator, Sir Arthur Conan Doyle, gave this explanation when he was interviewed late in life:

'I was quite a young doctor at the time. I had of course a scientific training, and I used occasionally to read detective stories. But it had always annoyed me that in the old-fashioned detective story the detective always seemed to get his results either by some sort of lucky chance or fluke - or else it was quite unexplained how he got there. ... It seemed to me that he's bound to give his reasons why he came to his conclusions. Well, when I began to think about this, I began to think of turning scientific methods, as it were, on the work of detection. And I used to have an old professor - his name was Bell - who was extraordinarly quick at detective work. He would look at the patient, he would hardly allow the patient to open his mouth, but he would make his diagnosis of the disease and also of the patient's nationality, and occupation and other points - entirely by his power of observation.'

Activity 8 (continued)

The opening of the story *The Red-readed League* shows this method very clearly. As so often in a Sherlock Holmes story, a visitor arrives at his rooms in 221B Baker Street with a problem.

The portly client puffed out his chest with an appearance of some little pride, and pulled a dirty and wrinkled newspaper from the inside pocket of his greatcoat. As he glanced down the advertisement column, with his head thrust forward, and the paper flattened out on his knee, I took a good look at the man, and endeavoured after the fashion of my companion to read the indications which might be presented by his dress or appearance.

I did not gain very much, however, by my inspection. Our visitor bore every mark of being an average commonplace British tradesman, obese, pompous and slow. He wore rather baggy grey shepherds' check trousers, a not over-clean black frock-coat, unbuttoned in the front, and a drab waistcoat with a heavy brassy Albert chain, and a square pierced bit of metal dangling down as an ornament. A frayed top hat, and a faded brown overcoat with a wrinkled velvet collar lay upon a chair beside him. Altogether, look as I would, there was nothing remarkable about the man save his blazing red head, and the expression of extreme chagrin and discontent upon his features.

Sherlock Holmes' quick eye took in my occupation and he shook his head with a smile as he noticed my questioning glances. 'Beyond the obvious facts that he has at some time done manual labour, that he takes snuff, that he is a Freemason, that he has been in China, and that he has done a considerable amount of writing lately, I can deduce nothing else.'

Mr Jabez Wilson started up in his chair, with his forefinger upon the paper, but his eyes upon my companion.

'How, in the name of good fortune, did you know that, Mr Holmes?' he asked. 'How did you know, for example, that I did manual labour? It's true as gospel, and I began as a ship's carpenter.'

'Your hands, my dear sir. Your right hand is quite a size larger than your left. You have worked with it, and the muscles are more developed.'

'Well, the snuff, then, and the Freemasonry?'

'I won't insult your intelligence by telling you that, especially as, rather against the strict rules of your order, you use an arc and compass breastpin.'

'Ah, of course, I forgot that. But the writing?'

'What else can be indicated by that right cuff so very shiny for five inches, and the left one with the smooth patch near the elbow where you rest it upon the desk.'

'Well, but China?'

'The fish which you have tattooed immediately above your right wrist could only have been done in China. I have made a small study of tattoo marks and have even contributed to the literature of the subject. That trick of staining the fishes' scales of a delicate pink is quite peculiar to China. When, in addition, I see a Chinese coin hanging from your watch-chain, the matter becomes even more simple.'

Mr Jabez Wilson laughed heavily. 'Well, I never!' said he. 'I thought at first you had done something clever, but I see that there was nothing in it after all.'

From *The Red-headed League*, Arthur Conan Doyle

Activity 9

'But, Holmes, I don't understand...'

Almost all of the many Sherlock Holmes stories are told by Dr Watson from his notes. Watson records the detective feats of his friend with admiration and in this he is, of course, like us the reader. Conan Doyle made sure that at the end of the story the reader had everything explained because Watson too needed everything made clear to him. The final sequence of many of the stories begins something like this:

'But Holmes, I don't understand. How did you know that...?' Holmes will then patiently explain - for Watson and for us!

Many writers since Conan Doyle have used two characters in this way. The most celebrated recent example is Colin Dexter in his stories of Inspector Morse and Sergeant Lewis. Can you think of other examples you have come across, in books or on screen?

The role of the two characters is clear – one is the expert and one the more ordinary assistant. In both examples Watson and Lewis act as 'foils' to the great detectives. In these stories, the reader can be halfway in their understanding of the great detective and his less intelligent assistant. As the writer well knows, this makes the reader feel much more confident about their ability to solve the crime!

But, to make it more interesting for the reader, it is never as simple as this. It is not that one character is clever and the other stupid. Writers create more complex detective partnerships than this so that we stay interested in these characters as people. The clever expert may have weaknesses in his or her character; the less intelligent assistant will almost certainly have other strengths. Can you see this in fictional detective partnerships that you know about?

Working with a partner, use your workbook or the box below to create two lists. The first column will show some characteristics of great detectives in partnerships that you know from stories or screen. The second will list the characteristics of their 'partner in crime'. Display, discuss and compare the lists with those of others. What do you notice?

Activity 10

Looking for clues

The final writing activity in Chapter 6 is the most ambitious one you will have worked on so far. You will need to use *all* the new skills you have learned in the Activities of *How to Teach Fiction Writing at Key Stage 3*.

Your task is to write a detective story using all that you have learned about writing so far. It is important to do two things at this stage:

- Review all the notes you have made so far in your workbook or in the appropriate boxes in this book.
- Follow the guidance given below about how to structure your narrative.

How to make your detective story work: use the series of steps below to plan the writing of your narrative.

Step 1

The most important starting point is your plot. There are some alternatives at this point. You could:

- Take a plot from an existing story - even a Sherlock Holmes one – and update it. A good Sherlock Holmes story to take would be *The Speckled Band*. It is a classic 'murder in a sealed room' story! With this approach, you keep the structure but update the settings and the characters.
- Develop one of the ideas you have come across in this book. For this approach, you are retelling the story as a crime to be solved. For example, two detectives are investigating sightings of a young girl seen at the entrance to the Mersey Tunnel . . .
- Use a real crime that you have heard about recently – in a paper, on the news, in a magazine – and set your detective story around these events. Build up a series of ideas from other sources and create a frame for your detective narrative. But do not use this approach unless you have some good ideas already.

The first of these is the easiest, the last the most difficult.

Step 2

Look at the final page of this Activity, which shows a CAD flow chart. This will help you to plan the Characters, Action and Description of your narrative. Use the CAD plan to make some basic notes about how your story will develop. Make sure that at this point you know the ending – who committed the crime and why! Look again at the points made in this chapter about the techniques that writers use. Refer back to your notes. If you have some ideas about setting and atmosphere, jot these down too.

Activity 10 (continued)

Step 3

Start to think about the two detective characters you are going to use. Use the character-building techniques from earlier chapters to help you. Ask some questions about your characters that help to build them up in your mind. Remember that you are creating a partnership between two people: it is not simply that one character is clever and the other is not!

Take some of the characteristics from your lists in Activity 9 to help you.

Step 4

Plan and write a key section of the narrative to see how it looks. Take a section in which the two main characters discover together some key aspect of the crime and then discuss how this moves their investigation forward.

Write no more than 400 words. Now review what you have written. Have you created two distinctive characters? Share your character creations with a partner. How might you improve what you have written?

Step 5

At this point, you are ready to begin your narrative! Check again through any notes you have made and make sure that your CAD plan is clear and complete before you begin.

Off you go!

Activity 10 (continued)

Start with the Action column – this is the outline of the plot. Then add notes about the Characters and the Descriptions. The arrows indicate how the characters and descriptions can 'feel into' and develop the plot.

CAD – Character, Action, Description!		
Character	Action	Description
	→ ←	
	→ ←	

© Neil MacRae ISBN 1-85346-858-4